John Rogers Bolles

The Gates of Hell Ajar

John Rogers Bolles

The Gates of Hell Ajar

ISBN/EAN: 9783743308718

Manufactured in Europe, USA, Canada, Australia, Japa

Cover: Foto ©ninafisch / pixelio.de

Manufactured and distributed by brebook publishing software (www.brebook.com)

John Rogers Bolles

The Gates of Hell Ajar

The Gates of Hell Ajar

John R. Bolles

JOHN R. BOLLES.

THE
GATES OF HELL AJAR,

—BY—

JOHN R. BOLLES.

Go, angel, go, at God's command,
Thy trumpet blow through all the land,
Till in the east the morning break,
And earth shall from its sleep awake,
Till Eden's paths again be trod,
And man shall walk and talk with God.

NEW LONDON, CONN.

Copyright, 1894, by John R. Bolles.

PROLOGUE.

When I think of the crime referred to in these pages, its disregard of law, human and divine, an insult to the Author of our being, a despite to nature itself, and when I think what God has done to adorn and glorify humanity, and of the sacred relation of marital life, ordained in the garden of Eden, honored and blest by His Son, type of heaven, I cannot doubt that the lowest depth of depravity has been reached.

The deliberate destruction of one, by those whom God has appointed, with the tenderest ties, to be its guardians and defenders! Blasted be the heart in which such a thought could spring! Smitten be the lips that would hint such a suggestion! Night has no darkness to cover the deed. Ordinary devils are ashamed of them, only the great red dragon, whose tail drew the third part of the stars of heaven, and did cast them to the earth can compare with these monsters in sin!

They take precedence. He stood before the

woman ready to devour the child as soon as it was born. They do not wait so long. They make haste to shed blood. What will be their doom when the judgment is set, when the books are opened, when God shall arise to shake terribly the earth? Nature is His common law, the Bible is His statute book.

Christianity does not repeal but affirms the law of retribution.

By our deeds we shall be judged. His fan is in His hand and He will thoroughly purge His floor, and gather the wheat into His garner, but He will burn up the chaff with unquenchable fire.

If our religion does not inspire reverence for the laws of God what is it good for? For saving souls? This is the Servonian bog into which the church is sinking. Not in, but from sin, is the promised salvation. Cry aloud, spare not, lift up thy voice like a trumpet, and show my people their transgressions, and the house of Jacob their sins.

"When God created the heavens and the earth, He divided the light from the darkness." As our hearts are linked with His the light will shine into them, we shall love righteousness and hate iniquity. We shall have no fellowship with the unfruitful works of darkness, but rather reprove them. This Agag of crime, that has made women childless, against which nature complains, and all true hearts testify. Let it be hewn in pieces, cursed with a curse, covered with shame. Let it be buried with the burial of an ass, drawn out and cast forth beyond the gates of Jerusalem.

There is no crime so fearful of detection as the one of which I speak. Like a hyena it walks the waste places of earth, it lurks in the shadow of death. Its wrath is hottest, because it is nearest to hell. The chambers of imagery seen by the prophet revealed no such abomination. Immortality is assailed. Love is contemned. Beauty is slain. Upon this Gilboa let there be no dew. The indifference manifested towards it is as appalling as the crime itself. Religion blanches not in its presence, or the gates of the church would be bolted against it, as are the gates of heaven.

The neck of the warhorse is clothed with thunder, but we attack sin with a flag of truce in our hand. Devoid of conscience, self-respect, natural affection, and every noble thought, these wretched criminals, though they may step upon pavements of gold, and flaunt their purple to the sun, have cast away the law of the Lord. The spotted garment they do not hate. They have withdrawn from all that is lovely, pure, and of good report, to bear the curse and wear the mark of Cain forever.

Look at the pallid face, the leprous blotch, the fetid breath. Are these not portents of the fate reserved for this transgression? It is arraigned at the bar. As it has shown no pity, let no pity be shown. Unlisped prayers ask that sentence be passed upon it.

> Panther of hell, escaped away,
> To make of human souls a prey!

Pestilence that walketh in darkness! It is a praise to language it has no word to express the vileness of the deed. Nature abhors it. Let it be an abhorring of all flesh.

Stars in your courses fight against it! Lightnings chase it! Bottomless pit, swallow it up and all that pertains to it. Let earth be freed from its stain. Let it be as though it had not been. Let a new heaven and a new earth be made, wherein shall dwell righteousness. Incense shall be offered unto love, and a pure offering. Blessed be the glory of the Lord from His place.

MY PRAYER.

O God! The Author of all good, the Hater of all wrong! There is no God with Thee. Thou liftest up Thy hand to heaven and sayest, I live forever! Whet Thy glittering sword, and let Thy hand take hold on judgment. Render vengeance to Thine enemies, and reward them that hate Thee. Let them that love Thee, be as the sun, when he goeth forth in his might. Let them be like a tree planted by the rivers of water, which bringeth forth its fruit in its season, and whose leaf shall not wither. Teach me to love what Thou lovest; to hate what Thou hatest, that I may be one with Thee, who cannot look upon sin. Teach me to do Thy will, to glorify Thee, in body, soul and spirit, which are Thine. Thou art a man of war; go forth with Thy servant to battle against the murderous hosts who contemn Thy laws, and defy Thy judgments; in whose skirts is the blood of poor innocents, and in their right hand a lie! Make me unto this people a fenced, brazen wall. Though they shall fight against me, let them not prevail against me, and let this work bring good to the world!

THE GATES OF HELL AJAR

BOOK I.

When God revealed His wondrous plan,
In His own image fashioned man,
The crowning gem of heaven's thought,
Then, woman to his hand was brought,
To be his glory and delight.
The stars were vocal at the sight'
Adorned with purity and grace
To be the mother of a race.
A race for which the world was made
And splendor of the sun displayed,
And to it sent, from God above,
The brightest token of his love,
Nature her great Creator saw,
And all but man obeyed His law.

To raise him from his lost estate,
By touch of sin made desolate,

Lo! Mercy flies on swiftest wing,
And shepherds hear the angels sing.
Wise men bring gold and incense sweet,
And worship at Immanuel's feet.

Beheld in God's beloved Son
The human and divine are one,
Since heaven for man has done its best,
To make him holy, happy, blest.
So sin, perhaps, has done its worst,
That he should be the most accursed
Sin, sin, how canst thou breathe the air,
When God has made all things so fair?
When every leaf with grace is bent,
And every bud is eloquent!

The mountain peaks that touch the sky,
The valleys that beneath them lie,
The white clouds floating on the air,
The lakelet girt with lilies fair,
The golden sunset, break of day,
The starry hosts, the milky way,
The forest depths, the autumn's glow.

The rainbow tints, the flakes of snow
All things below, all things above,
Teach us obedience and love.

O Source of Beauty, Source of Light.
Unveil Thy glory to my sight,
That I for truth may ever stand,
A faithful witness in the land.
I would not seek on hills to tread,
With dainty violets o'erspread.
On meadows sweet with lilies flecked,
On fields with dandelions decked,
Through scented paths or sparkling lawn,
Robed with the blushes of the morn.
Nor would I pace the halls of state
To mingle with the honored great.
I ask to hurl Ithuriel's spear,
To make my thoughts to mortals clear;
I ask to soar on lofty wing,
To dip my pen in truth's pure spring.
To wait, my God, on Thee alone,
And take my orders from Thy throne!
Make Thou my heart as lion strong

To tell of right and tell of wrong,
To wield Thy word with holy grace,
To flash its blade in Satan's face
And pierce him in his hiding place.

There is a deed of darkness done,
On this fair earth beneath the sun,
Conceived within the foulest cell
Of that dread region we call hell.
No tongue can speak, no pen can paint
Its leprosy, its moral taint.
Sword that is bathed in heaven, red,
Idumea's sword light on its head '
Ye fiery billows o'er it roar,
And sink it that it rise no more !
It sweeps the stars of heaven away :
It makes of unborn souls a prey.
Its punishment let no one stay,
Anathema, Maranatha !
O sun, O moon, withdraw your light,
O stars, conceal your faces bright!
To depth of degradation brought,
And infamy surpassing thought.

Of such a one what shall I say?
Who hastes to snatch young life away,
Lest it should see the purpling dawn,
Or drink the pure, sweet breath of morn,
Or lay its head upon thy breast,
Thou hideous one, thou devil's best!
My hate of thee shall ever stand
A fadeless jewel on my hand.
Engraven as by heavenly art,
I press it closely to my heart,
And offer thanks to God above
That I can hate as well as love.

The ostrich of the wilderness,
That bears her head with pride,
Hardening herself against her young,
Of wisdom's gift denied ;
Or she whose forehead knows no shame
And cannot blush, I hide the name,
Are as white angels by thy side.
Since first the morning stars were heard,
No savage beast, no ravenous bird,
Has done a deed like thine.

The serpent crawls, and eats the dust,
But thou art more than he accursed,
    And of a baser line.
Hell from beneath is moved to meet,
The rapid coming of thy feet.

Silence forever cover thee !
To strike from immortality
The bright celestial flame,
To spare not even thine own blood,
Thou trampler on the laws of God,
Unspoken be thy name !
See, hissing serpents around thee twine !
Medusa's head and crown are thine.

What fittest word shall I employ?
To curse the crime ; or praise the joy
From pure and holy love that springs,
Where broods the dove with stainless wings,
And fondest hopes in beauty smile,
Like flowerets from a blessed isle.

Lo ! the fair angels take their flight
Down from the realms above,

And close beside a mother, light,
To bless a mother's love ;
The bat that 'round thy pillow flies,
Points where a moral ruin lies ;
'Tis there the screech-owl builds her nest,
The great owl finds a place of rest.
How art thou fallen, wearing thy chain,
Cast down and wounded, how art thou slain !

To sell a mother from her child !
And Christian eyes look on and smiled.
Oh ! slavery, smitten by His rod,
And withering 'neath the wrath of God !
But thou a lower depth hast sought,
Unfathomed by the reach of thought.
Lost to all sense of self-respect,
So near to hell art thou,
Its molten waves thy face reflect,
Its seal is on thy brow,
Thy crime, with damning colors set,
Has not on earth its equal met !
Give me, O God, the axe of truth,
To lay it at its root ;

And let the fire unquenchable,
Comsume it branch and shoot.

A twofold criminal thou shalt
In infamy abide ;
And wear the mark blacker than Cain's,
Of murder, suicide.
Oh ! wretch, the one you slay might save
Your life, or soothe you to the grave.

Our bodies fashioned by His hand
Are temples of the Lord ;
All who defile them He'll destroy,
So speaks His holy word.

There might have been one warbler more,
Which to thine ear had sung ;
The tree that's silent by the door,
With music might have rung.
Who gives to thee complacent look,
Is blotted out of life's fair book.

Ye startled lightnings, find a path
To tell the story of your wrath !
A mother's deed, I speak with shame
Of one not worthy of the name,
So base, unhallowed, impious,
The world has not an equal curse.
Not blight, nor rotteness, nor death,
Nor leprous glare, nor poisonous breath,
Not all the ills upon thee sent,
Fruit of thy crime and punishment.
With murder written on thy soul,
I see thee stand at hell's dark goal,
Complete embodiment of sin !
Gapes wide its mouth to take thee in !

Had'st thou but known, in this thy day,
What to thy peace belongs,
Redeemed thou had'st to Zion come,
Upon thy lips her songs.
A crown of everlasting joy,
Were set upon thy head ;
Now a full cup of bitterness
Is given thee instead.

What of the father shall we say,
Who like a gaunt wolf prowls around,
As if some new born joy he'd found,
When infant life is cast away.
Oh! by what word can tongue express
The summit of thy wickedness!
Hyena lurking 'mongst the dead!
In him are all vile things concentered,
And into him all devils entered.
Epitome of hell is he,
Of hell on earth and infamy.
Begone, O monster, thou hast fed,
On blood, until thine eyes are red!
Hell cannot wait till thou art there,
Who thine own offspring didst not spare!

You, you have insulted the Author of all;
The sword of His vengeance is lifted to fall!
The waves of His justice shall flow on forever,
And out of His hand there is none can deliver.

Oh! when I think what God has done,
For human happiness,

To open up within the soul,
Such founts of joy and bliss,
Sweet and clear from life's pure river,
Flowing from the throne forever ;
And when I think what sin has wrought,
And of the smoking pit,
I wonder not the angel cast
That dragon into it.

And they who step the church within,
To hide the blotches of their sin,
Are dragons now in embryo,
And know the place to which they go.

But what for those who have no frown,
When heaven's high law is trodden down?
No eye to see the flaming sword
That executes the wrath of God,
Who find more beauty to admire
In sin than in the prophet's ire ;
Hug the vile adder to their breast,
And soothe him to his quiet rest,
 "So fair, so gentle and so good,"

While his forked tongue is red with blood !
Who heed not when the mountain shakes !
Nor tremble when Jehovah speaks.
They'd stone St. Paul if he were here
And with their guilt should interfere.
Break Sinai's law in pieces too,
To get the stones they hurl at you,
Tables which God's own finger drew ;
Yet think they stand at heaven's gate
And for their entrance angels wait.
Oh ! Prophet, come and heal the spring,
The holy salt into it fling !

Is it nothing to you, all ye that pass by,
When the infant is lifting its mournful cry
For life? That the murderer's hand may be stayed?
Will you smile at the crime, will you lend it your aid?

   The glory transcendent
   That shines out between
   The gates so resplendent,
   Their eyes have not seen.

One glimpse of his beauty,
One sight of the King,
They'd offer him incense,
A pure offering.

The snow-white doves have taken flight,
The buzzards round about them light.
As they who look on Virtue's face
Win the enchantment of her grace ;
So sin of us becomes a part
If we but clasp it to our heart,
A horrid serpent to us grown,
Or by its touch we're turned to stone.

O Jesus, I behold in Thee
All beauty, grace and purity,
But deeds are done in Thy blest name,
Which mantle earth and heaven with shame.

Still let me by Thy precepts live
And watch my steps with care,
And let me not insult Thy name,
With murder and with prayer.

But know the darkness from the light,
The bitter from the sweet,
And ever keep within my sight
The footprints of Thy feet.

"What wounds are these upon Thy hands?"
"I got them not in heathen lands,
In my friends' house they're given me,
The print of nails and blood you see?"

When will mankind discern the truth,
Taught clearly in His word,
That without holiness no man
Shall ever see the Lord?

"The devils think that they are fair,"
So Swedenborg once said,
"And there are those in hades now
Who do not know they're dead."

"Naked and poor, and blind indeed,
Thou sayest I'm rich and nothing need!"

"I counsel thee to buy fine gold,
And raiment white of me,
With eye-salve to anoint thine eyes,
That thou mayst clearly see!"
So speaks the High and Holy One,
Whose countenance is as the sun.

Call evil good, make no complaint
Of sin, you are a model saint.
For Satan set a cushioned seat,
And pleasant words to him repeat,
You'll be as beauteous to behold
As wings of dove all silvered o'er,
Her feathers laid with yellow gold ;
Do this and you need do no more.
Among the saints you'll stand confessed,
Shoulders and head above the rest.
But should you plead God's law instead,
Herodias' daughter takes your head !

Mark the religious charlatan,
Who vaunts himself a righteous man,

Puts on his sanctimonious airs,
And whines in nasal tones his prayers,
Yet will not hesitate to do
What common sinners would eschew.
And when he turns his hand to steal
Has but to show the greater zeal.
Rend thou his borrowed fleece away,
A full sized wolf thou wilt display.

The toad that squat close to the ear
Of Eve, touched by Ithuriel's spear,
Sprang up a fiend of horrid mien ;
And many such like toads are seen.

There came a prophet of the Lord
From Judah, to proclaim His word,
He stood and 'gainst the altar cried,
With Jereboam by His side,
"O altar, altar!"   So we cry
Where incense false ascends on high.

When Israel came from Egypt's land,
Jehovah took him by the hand,
And bade him all His statutes do,
He sinned and God the people slew.

How is it in the gospel day?
" Now love bears rule," I hear one say!
Would you caress a cruel child,
Or turn your prisoners all out wild,
Upon society to prey?
Such love as that be cast away!
It for the anarchist will plead,
Cover with praise the bloody deed.
Love has a higher ministry,
It pleads for law and equity,
It is the soul of chastity.
It will not palliate the wrong,
For God and truth it standeth strong.
The noblest flowering of the mind,
'Tis wisdom, goodness, truth combined.
When Satan tries to be a saint
He's the worst subject we can paint,
Transformed he has e'en less of grace

Than when he shows his natural face.
Let Satan masked with love bear sway
Sin has its Pentecostal day.
But well I know, early or late,
That God His laws will vindicate.
And that the sword that longest waits
Is brightest burnished by the Fates.
And I do solemnly aver,
Annihilation I'd prefer,
Than be the walls of heaven within,
Were God to take no note of sin.
The farthest star would cease to burn,
The universe to chaos turn!
"Though I," the great apostle said,
"Or a bright angel in my stead,
Should any other gospel preach,
Or any other doctrine teach,
Than I have preached from the first,
Let him forever be accursed."

We praise the Author of all good
For countless mercies shown,

For pure religion's blessed tie,
Which binds us to His throne,
And for the law, so holy, just,
He has to us made known.

THE GATES OF HELL AJAR.

BOOK II.

I lift my voice in the defence
Of helpless, speechless innocents.
I plead humanity's great cause,
And ask obedience to God's laws,
So clearly written by His hand
That all who read may understand.
I plead against the foulest crime
That ever shocked the ear of time,
And still the heaviest chain doth wear
In outer darkness and despair ;
For meanness most unparalleled,
By Satan's grasp most firmly held.
I plead for God and His great name,
The Source from whence our being came,
I plead for beauty, truth and grace,
For honor and the human race.

I plead for love with lips aflame !
And I would hurl my javelin
Into the heart of this one sin,
Its infamy proclaim.

The ire of God may seem to sleep,
But dreadful is the pause
Ere from His hand the lightnings leap
To glorify His laws.
Weep, howl forever and lament !
You walk a fearful road
For you have a forerunner sent
To plead 'gainst you with God.

You've reared aloft your serpent crest,
You've fed on human life ;
Before the world you stand confessed,
Devil and devil's wife.

The praise of serpents shall be sung,
For they protect and guard their young,
And Sodom shall in judgment stand
Witness against a Christian land.

Could I but speak in words so clear,
So near akin to heaven,
That angels should stoop down to hear
The thoughts to mortal given,
I'd magnify the truth of God
That holds o'er sin a burning rod!
And I would show in many a saint
A sepulchre made white with paint.
The pearl of price is sought by few,
A glassy counterfeit will do,
And passes at a premium, too!
And they who love and make a lie
Are sportful as a butterfly
That scatters round its baneful brood,
Destroying all that's green and good.

Arm me, O God, with Thy whole mind,
To set Thy law before mankind,
Teach me to sound truth's clarion well,
To ring aloud the heavenly bell,
That the words that I shall speak
May be all in sweet accord

With the beauty of the Earth
And the glory of the Lord.
And let me still Thy truth declare
Whether they hear me or forbear ;
And not one single jot abate
To win their love or shun their hate.

As God doth human souls refine
He makes in them His glory shine,
And when each sinful stain has flown
We are to His own image grown.
Who glorifies His holy name
And lights in us the hallowed flame ;
And love, held from its throne too long,
Is pure as the Archangel's song.

I throw myself into the breach
Like him of ancient Rome.
This mighty gulf must be closed up
Or Earth has met its doom.

I will battle with the tempest
When I know that I am right,

The thunder and the lightning
Shall be nothing in my sight.

I will fight the powers of evil
Till every one submit,
And serve upon the devil
A warrant for the pit.

I care not what the world shall think,
The world too long has slept.
I care not what the church may blink,
Its vineyard is not kept.

See! Virtue in thy pillared halls
Is timid to appear,
And pride struts lofty on thy walls,
A mocking chanticleer.

Within thy gates the siren sings,
Vice finds a shelter 'neath thy wings.
And should one dare to speak out bold
Like rapt Isaiah, prophet of old,
Who cried aloud, t'would be no wonder
If he like him were sawn asunder.

'Tis with no common modes of thought
That I to meet this foe am brought,
With sword and spear and blunderbuss
I fight the beasts at Ephesus.

Give all your goods to feed the poor,
It is not worth a pin
While sin stands usher at your door
To welcome murder in.

Earth cannot hide such monster guilt
Though sun and moon retire ;
For every drop of blood thus spilt
There waits a day of ire.

God's judgments are a mighty deep :
We cannot look so far.
We see the path our feet should keep,
We see our guiding star.

Shall we lay up a dreadful store
Of vengeance for that day,
Of wrath against the day of wrath,
Or walk the shining way ?
Come out of her, my people, come,

As Lot from Sodom went,
Tarry ye not in all the plain,
You're to the mountain sent.

No church shall call me to account,
I stand on Zion's holy mount.
I stand alone, my God, with Thee,
Who evermore will stand by me.
With sling-stones from the brook of Truth,
I in Thy name will go ;
So David, but a ruddy youth,
Laid the proud giant low.
And I will be as strong in Thee,
My hair as white as snow.

What from the temple do we hear?
An awful stillness fills the air.
Silence is reigning everywhere,
Silence as when an earthquake's near.

"Declare smooth things," the people say.
The preacher answers, "I obey.
For I to you as one am sent
That playeth on an instrument."

No John the Baptist's voice is heard,
No prophet's holy anger stirred,
No Jeremiah's lamentation
Awakes the slumbers of a nation,
None sigh for the abomination.
Religion's car, like Juggernaut,
Crushes these souls without a thought ;
Souls, which beneath the altar cry,
'' How long, O Lord, O Lord most high !

The watchmen look it in the face,
And turn away with saintly air
As if no skeleton were there ;
This cancer on the human race !

Religion of the present day
Is like a blossom blown away ;
It leaves no fruit upon the stem,
It does not touch the Saviour's hem.
It wears no royal diadem !
No bible precept by it taught,
And with no sense of duty fraught,

It does not know that it is dead,
And flowers upon its coffin spread.
But there are seven thousand now
Who do not unto Baal bow.

Gird, gird thy sword upon thy thigh,
O thou, most mighty, ride,
Ride prosperously, with meekness, truth,
Attendant by thy side.
Because thou lovest righteousness,
And hatest sin in every dress,
With perfumed garments clad,
Therefore hath God anointed thee
With oil of gladness copiously,
Out of the ivory palaces,
Whereby thou art made glad.

Religion set from hate apart
Like the swamp apple has no heart,
It is a fungus growth indeed,
And bears within no living seed.
Ye angels from above look down,
Whose faces never wore a frown.

"Ne'er wore a frown? It is not true,
For we can hate as well as you."
'Twas thus the swift responses flew.
Another cried at heaven's gate,
" 'Tis beautiful that we can hate,"
Hate evil ye that love the Lord,
Hate dwells with love in blest accord,
And without hatred all invain
We seek perfection to attain.
It is an attribute of God,
And, therefore, should be mine,
Or in His image, clear and pure,
My soul could never shine.

Did I not hate a dastard thing,
Meanness, with all my might,
I could not drink from the pure spring
Of truth, of honor bright.

And falsehood's base and rancorous brood,
Which fly about to sting,
Were innocent and beautiful
As bird of starry wing.

O blessed, holy, virtue, hate !
Dwell in my heart in royal state,
A glory fair, sent from above,
That I may truly learn to love.

The dingy bat, the oriole bright,
Are of one color in the night,
'Tis so where moral darkness reigns,
'Twixt right and wrong no sign remains.

Say God hates not iniquity !
We plead for infidelity,
We make of bible truth a lie !
From the bright sun we turn our eye.
Like vines in cellars shut from light,
We're puny, weak, and sickly white.
The red, the blue, the green, the gold,
Their splendors to the sun unfold.

In the rift of the rock the fresh flowerets spring,
When the shadows are falling the nightingales
    sing,

On the bleak, snowy mountain the Edelweiss
    grows,
Midst sharpest of briars the sweet-scented rose,
From out the dark mold comes the blossom of
    beauty,
So hatred of sin is the groundwork of duty.

It is because we will not part
With sin to gain a holy heart,
That we for love such sticklers are,
And not for purity most fair.

The stars above their gifts dispense,
Centres of light and influence,
Destroy the central force, there'd be
No universe such as we see.
Destroy the grand, diffusive power,
The world were darkness from that hour.
In beauteous harmony combined
All things reflect the human mind.
O beauty, virtue's sister sweet,
I pay my homage at thy feet!

Wave, wave o'er earth thy roseate wing,
Stars in your heavenly courses sing.
O truth, unveil thy peerless face,
To lift from sin the human race,
And love, as white as angel's breast,
Invite to heaven's eternal rest!
If beauty, truth, will not inspire,
Let hail-stones fall and coals of fire!

God sends the sunshine and the rain,
Spreads glory on the hill and plain;
He bids the little buds to spring,
Gives to the bird its dappled wing;
Plants with His hand the forest trees,
But in the soul Himself He sees.
O might the echo of my thought
By seraph's tongue to earth be brought!
'Twould lend, perhaps, a listening ear,
And drop the penitential tear.
No sweeter strains from golden lyres
E'er flowed; than holy love inspires
Within the soul where beauty dwells,
And truth unseals its living wells.

My Father! Unto Thee I've cried!
Thou from my youth hast been my guide,
Didst Thou not send thine angel bright,
Cause to fly swiftly from the skies,
At time of evening sacrifice,
To point me up the stairs of light?
He bade me hearken to Thy voice,
And make obedience my choice,
And said Thou would'st not turn away,
To do me good now and for aye.
Thy promises I have believed
And all of good from Thee received.

When sadness marked my lonely way
And tears bedewed the earth,
In every place where dragons lay
Have risen songs of mirth,
A joy sprang up for every tear,
And gladness bloomed in place of fear.

As early with the dawning sweet,
I sought the distant wild retreat
To be with God alone;

His hand upon my head was pressed,
As child by parent is caressed,
My burden all had flown!

They that believe shall not make haste
But wait the moment bright,
When He will turn our griefs to joy,
Our darkness into light.

He makes the seven stars to rise,
Lays bold Orion on the skies,
And bids the Pleiades dispense
Over the world sweet influence,
Fresh as the drops of morning dew,
His mercies are forever new,
And cordials to our heart are sent,
To cheer us in our banishment.

I thank Thee, O Thou God of Love,
That earth and heaven have met,
As the glad sunshine from above
Is in the dewdrop set.

Would I put on a crown of gold,
And the whole world command,
Unless thou badest me to hold
The sceptre in my hand?

Though pleasant be the rays of light,
And sweet the sun to see,
I would not take the gift of sight
Did'st Thou not give it me!
Nor would I hold a secret spring
Of joy apart from Thee,
Who bid'st me drink from fountains bright,
Yea, drink abundantly.

When fearful thunders rend the air,
And nature quakes within,
I think how terrible His wrath,
Who cannot look on sin.

Instruction flows into my soul
From nature's sweeter words,
The fragrant fields, the murmuring rill,
The song of earliest birds.

I lift my thoughts up to the stars,
And in their eyes I see
That holy watchers from above
Are looking down on me.

I listen to the chiming bells,
I hear the words untold,
The lightsome touch of angels' feet
Around me I behold,
As left upon the flowerets sweet
That beauty's self infold.
And will they not forever bloom
In heaven itself, their native home?
Upon the quiet waters there
Shall peaceful lilies rest,
And glories lent to earth adorn
The mansions of the blest?
When sin with us no more is seen
There'll be no parting line between.

The traveler upon his way
Will sometimes stop awhile,

To gaze upon the pleasant things
That round about him smile.

The buttercups he'll not despise
That look up in his face,
Nor less the lily will he prize
That bends with modest grace.

Fancy leads him as he roves
Through her thickly-tented groves
Where the woodbines knit their loves :
And rules the fairy queen
With the waving of her wand
O'er the prankish elfin band,
Dancing on the green.
Trailing the arbutus sweet
For the touch of dainty feet
By the twilight seen.
Tripping to the water's brink
Where the willows bend to drink,
And the clouds that float the sky
Mirrored in its clear depths lie.

Wading for the curling cresses,
Gathering up their rainbow dresses,
Shaking out their airy tresses,
Where lights the butterfly.
And when the sun sinks down to rest
They weave for him a golden vest,
And sing his lullaby.
Listening to the katydid,
'Neath its leafy covert hid,
Nestling in their mossy bed,
Starlit curtains overspread,
The lotus blossom nigh ;
And first to hail the waking dawn,
They blow throughout their haunts the horn,
Then strike their tents and fly
To the weird and shadowy lake,
Fringed by willows, alders, brake,
Where their pastime fairies take,
Tip their wings in bubbling wells,
And hide within the lily-bells.

O Love, when thou didst step on earth,
Sweet messenger of heavenly birth,

Ere Adam sinned, or fell a tear,
Thou didst the songs of Eden hear,
But now thou tread'st on thorny ground,
And thy fair feet have many a wound.
Stay with us though the night be long
Till thou again hear Eden's song.

O pure is the violet's breath in the spring,
And sweet are the notes the bobolinks sing,
And white are the snow-flakes that light from
    above,
But purer, and sweeter, and whiter is love!
Blacker than the blackest night
Is the crime the gods would smite.

Pandora's box it is indeed,
From it all mischiefs rise,
It nourishes a monster breed,
Which earth and heaven defies.

If I but had his power of speech,
Who through the heavens flew,
The everlasting word to preach,
I'd tell the ghastly crew,

Vampires who slake with blood their thirst
Abhorred of men, of God accurst,
That I had seen the glittering spear,
Ready to pierce them through,
When mercy drops her final tear
And sighs her last adieu !

THE GATES OF HELL AJAR.

BOOK III.

The mills of God grind very slow
But grind exceeding small,
His flaming eyes are everywhere,
He sees and numbers all,
The eagle in its lofty flight,
The sparrow in its fall ;
And though the vision tarry late
His justice will not aught abate.

O muse, attune my waiting lyre,
Touch every string with holy fire,
That I may face this bold Goliah
That dares defy with lifted rod
The armies of the living God.
I will not sing of birds and flowers,
Of insects' wings and moonlit hours,

On other themes I'm bade to dwell,
My song shall be of heaven and hell
As seen upon the world below
Ere the Archangel's trump shall blow.
As seen when earth and sky shall flee
Away, and there is no more sea.
Hell lures with blandishment and smile,
The siren sings but to beguile ;
Heaven bids us die that we may live,
Immortal life we thus receive.
In nature it is also true
All things by death their lives renew.
O virtue holy, in thy face,
The brightest smile of God we trace !
Afflicted, tossed with tempest here,
A sapphire waits for every tear,
When thy foundations are displayed
With pleasant stones thy borders laid.
Decked with the tints of rosy morn
Fair colors shall thy walls adorn.
O vice, upon thy face is seen
The brand of hell without a screen.

Honor is like a bauble sold,
And innocence betrayed for gold.
Earth is a molten sea of sin,
If we look deep enough within.
Marriage, a holy, sacred rite,
Is profanation, moral blight,
In all who dare to violate
The sanctions of that blessed estate ;
And all who 'gainst their offspring rise,
Legitimate or otherwise,
Are doomed to meet the murderer's fate !
Not one in three, I have been told
By shrewd physicians, young and old,
Are left to see the light of day,
By these vile wretches thrust away
To fill the great Aceldama !
And should the line be drawn between
The church and world, 'tis scarcely seen.

Could I but wield an equal sling,
Made by the Cyclop's pattern,
The murderers every one I'd fling
Beyond the planet Saturn.

O God! if Thou hast words to give,
O give them unto me,
To show the house unto the house,
Chambers of imagery!

Call yourselves Christians? and look up
And drink from one communion cup.
Bring no more your vain oblation,
You to yourselves have drinked damnation.
Your new moons and your solemn feasts,
I hate with all my heart,
Salvation is a burning lamp
Enlightening every part,
Not a dead sea petrifaction
For crime to whet its blade upon.

Earth, cover not the blood that's spilt,
Hide not the blood-stained hand,
So much of crime, so much of guilt,
Strides o'er a weeping land,
Which like a mountain weight doth rest
"Peine forte et dure" upon its breast!
But men do not heed the boding signs,

The bristling movement of the lines,
The footsteps of the coming wrath,
The cyclone traveling on their path,
The jagged clouds for battle set,
The glittering spear for vengeance whet.
Then let the curtain be uplifted
And from the wheat the chaff be sifted.

That vice and crime in every land
Abashed before the world shall stand,
And virtue shed its sweetest rays
In glory set above all praise.

O Christ, when Thou didst walk the sea,
Thou madest there a path for me,
Be Thou forevermore my guide
And keep me always near Thy side.

Reproving evil, we're a prey,
The hounds of hell will at us bay ;
Pilate and Herod will unite,
High priest will be the first to smite.
Too good to step in Gentile hall
Yet crucify the Lord of all.

If there should be two devils out,
I give as my opinion,
The one that wore a Christian coat
Would hold the chief dominion.

Best things perverted are the worst,
And hypocrites the most accursed.
What is religion, do you say?
It is to hearken and obey,
To do the will of God below
As it is done in heaven above;
This is religion well I know,
This is the doctrine that I love.
It is the turning of the heart
To choose with Mary the good part;
It is the turning of the feet
To walk in wisdom's ways most sweet,
Not sitting on the anxious seat.

I tell a story, it is true,
There was a man whose name I knew,
Serious, no doubt, and half sincere,
He forward came and asked for prayer.

A stalwart man beside him knelt,
And as still more of zeal he felt
He gave the bench a harder blow,
For what offence we do not know ;
Then suddenly his fist came whack
Down on the anxious sinner's back,
And often did the blow repeat.
The poor man sprang upon his feet,
I've got it ! got it ! loud he cried.
Thanksgivings rose on every side.
He says it was his back to save
That he such testimony gave.

O that my pen had power to paint
The portrait of a real saint !
I'd dip it deep in truth's clear flame,
And if I could, I'd call the name.
Like Enoch here he walks with God,
Like Abraham believes His word,
In all his house he's faithful found,
Like Moses stands on holy ground.
Obedient to His command,
He takes the law from God's own hand ;

Like John he finds his sweetest rest
In leaning on his Savior's breast.
"Spring up, O well," we hear him sing,
Salvation's wells about him spring !
The angels watch him from the skies !
"Show me Thy ways," to God he cries.
He hears a word behind him say
"This is the true and living way."
God is his buckler and his shield,
He bids him fight but never yield.
The Lord among His saints shall stand,
And they shall dwell in Beulah land.

Monarch of infidelity,
Step forth that we thy face may see,
God's promise in the soul is great,
No word of His shall want its mate.
What bringest thou within thy hand
But empty shells from barren strand !
   O foolish one,
    The light to shun,
And into outer darkness run ;
What were the world without the sun ?

No bud of spring, no autumn leaf,
No bird to sing, no golden sheaf!
Enshrouded in eternal gloom,
Of beauty and of life the tomb.
Why choose to dwell in dismal mines
To search for fancied good,
When the great sun above us shines
And pours a golden flood?
Why shut against ourselves the door
By which we come to God ;
Presume to tell the Omniscient One
What He should do or leave undone?
Nor listen when the stars rehearse
The anthems of the universe?
Shall we impugn the aim and end
Of things we do not comprehend,
When there is set before our sight
All needful truths in letters bright?
Your words are stout against the Lord,
You've strown the seeds of death abroad,
"Vengeance is mine, I will repay."
You do not see the angel stand
Before you, with drawn sword in hand,

Omnipotent to slay!
You do not heed the words divine
That shall not pass away.
They "who shall fall upon that stone
Shall be broken, every one!
On whomsoever it shall fall
Him it will grind to powder small."
Why cast the Bible to the ground,
In which sublimest truth is found?
And why with ruthless hand efface
God's image from the human race?
His witnesses are everywhere,
In earth, and sea, and sky, and air,
The sunset hues, the stars that glow,
The flashing dews, the flakes of snow!
Are all things into being brought
Without creative power or thought?
A firefly's torch, a glow-worm's spark,
Only to leave the night more dark,
A surface shimmer on the sea
Is boastful Infidelity.

In a dark throne thou tak'st thy seat,

Not as a prophet to repeat
Great truths the soul to elevate,
Envenomed teacher of blind fate !
Rejecting all that's good and great,
Sowing the seed on every side
Of egotism, folly, pride.
Lost to high reason's blest control,
Lost to the logic of the soul.

Might I on wing seraphic soar
And truth's eternal realm explore,
I'd bring as much as arms could hold
Of diamonds, rubies, sapphires, gold,
And lay them at thy feet,
And sparkling rays of light so clear,
As tokens of a brighter sphere,
With song of angels sweet !
I'd bear thee up to heaven's gate,
Where the good angels watch and wait,
Repentance's tear to greet.
A change of raiment to thee given
And to thy lips the speech of heaven !

But thou shalt know the Nazarene
Will conquer, though by shaft unseen.

"Captain, I've left the star behind
By which you bade me steer,"
So said the boy, and this is done
By older ones, I fear.

We may not trust another star
Than that to us is given,
If we would safely guide our bark
Into the port of heaven.

Avoid the great in their own eyes,
Their Lilliputians in disguise,
And by the rule which never fails,
When weighed in truth's eternal scales,
Are less than those whom they despise.
Agrippa shone out like a star,
St. Paul was prisoner at the bar,
The man who builds the ship is great,
Who makes the engine go,
Who stirs the secret springs of thought,
That on forever flow ;

Who wisely guides the helm of state,
Not he who wears the crown is great,
But greatest he in heaven's sight
Who stands invincible for right.

Repel the flattering politician,
He'll cheat you worse than the magician,
Serve him, he vows to be your friend,
On whom you ever may depend ;
Ask him the smallest thing to do,
You'll find how much he thinks of you.
Chase not the ignis fatuus blaze
That lures with its deceitful rays.
But more than all of those beware
Who plume a high religious air,
Who claim to strike the heavenly lyre,
And sing among the angel choir,
And think they walk by Christian rule,
When they are stubborn as a mule ;
Forever right in their own sight,
Yet drink not at truth's fountain bright.
Who rush ahead with unwashed feet,
To tread upon the golden street.

From blest humility apart,
No heavenly thought springs in the heart.
The bird that flies on quickest wings
To heaven's gate, and sweetest sings,
Builds its nest in lowly places,
Emblem of true Christian graces.

A solemn look and measured tone
Are signs by which a rogue is known.
The honest man no vizor wears,
His words are few and short his prayers.

A thousand errors spring around,
Like mists from miasmatic ground,
The baneful vapors of the night,
The sun dispels them with his light.
They who reject the Bible story
Of Jesus' birth, the Lord of glory,
Have nowhere that their feet may stand,
They build their house upon the sand ;
The winds shall sweep it all away,
'Twill not be found at the last day.

When you behold a saintly show
With bearing of the head so low,
And on the lips a smile so sweet,
Ready with pious words to greet,
Be sure a hypocrite you meet.
And when you hear a voice too bland,
Beware of Esau's hairy hand.

There is a love in weakness set,
Of goodness the base counterfeit,
For sin it has as sweet a word
As e'er was sung by mother bird.
All mischiefs in its presence thrive,
As rankest worms on carrion live.
Far more than hate it doth devour ;
With no reproof from childhood's hour,
One always would have his own way.
Thus coming up without a head
He took on him a wolf's instead,
And so became a beast of pray.
Not an exception to the rule,
He culminated in a fool.

Eli, who seemed to be a saint,
Over his sons held no restraint,
Hophni and Phineas are slain,
And none of Eli's house remain.

Too much indulgence we should know
With even justice does not go,
And in whatever form displayed
Is not on truth's foundation laid.
Ten thousand ills which curse the earth
From this vile parentage have birth.
It hatches out a lazy bird
Like that which we are told
Tosses the others from their nest
That it the nest may hold.

Nature has nothing more to say
Of meanness done in meanest way,
Because she never could excel
The picture she has drawn so well.
Still she reveals her wondrous lines,
On every page instruction shines.

Lines of beauty, veins of gold,
Diamonds which their light infold,
Ready to send out the rays
Kindled by the soul's pure blaze.
Nature speaks to every one,
In the rising, setting sun,
In the singing of the bird,
In the stillness never heard,
In the violets 'bout our feet,
In the breath of morning sweet,
In the colors of the bow,
In the whiteness of the snow,
In the flower that blooms alone,
Only to its Maker known.
We note upon the robin's breast
A parent's tender love expressed.

In the chameleon we may find
The type of an unstable mind.
All that is beautiful and sweet
We shall in heart and life repeat ;
All that is ugly we shall hate,

Nor for a moment imitate.
'Tis thus by love and hate we rise
To gain fair virtue's lofty prize.
Could I within thy temple raise
A tribute, nature, to thy praise,
Silence should guide my worship then,
And silence breathe its deep amen !

At fashion I would strike a blow,
Society that's high is low.
Extremes are often known to meet,
The east and west each other greet.
What gem of beauty hast thou set
Upon a mother's coronet ?
A cloud of everlasting shame
Shall lie upon their breast,
Whose hands with blood of innocents
Have dyed their purple vest.

O love, the clearest cup of joy
That human lips can taste,
How is thy home made desolate,
Thy palaces laid waste !

Pure as the snow on mountain driven
And roseate as the blush of day,
Love, love, the choicest pearl of heaven,
How art thou vilely cast away !

Let now some heavenly archer stand
Close by my side to guide my hand,
That every arrow by me sent
Shall go from bow Omnipotent.

"It is not right," you may have said,
The hornet flies about your head.
The demon stands upon your path
As the quick messenger of wrath,
Red-hot and of a brimstone smell,
The latest emigrant from hell.
Its fire is flashing from his eyes,
"You have insulted me," he cries.
'Twas then I vowed that I would make
The walls of Satan's kingdom shake
And to their dark foundations quake.
Before I'd fought him from afar ;
Now, hand to hand, I am for war.

I will uncover this deep pit
And bring it out to sight,
And God, who calls me to the work,
Shall clothe me with His might.
And all the festering, hissing brood
I, in His name, will smite ;
And still I will my sword unsheathe,
And keep my armor bright,
Until not one be left to breathe,
This progeny of night !

The scorner's wrath is very hot,
Reprove him, you will get a blot,
With hardened neck he'll onward go
'Till he receive the fatal blow.
'Twill light upon him suddenly,
Destroyed and without remedy.

Still from the mount of prophecy
I'd pay a tribute, love, to thee ;
Fair as the dew that fell of yore
On Hermon, blest forevermore !

My heart rejoices to behold
A man more precious than fine gold.
A woman, too, appears in sight
With heavenly radiance bedight,
Woman in all her pristine grace
Like the first mother of our race,
The latest thought of heaven expressed,
The beauty of the world confessed.
I see them at the altar stand
And take each other by the hand.
God's holy ordinance is blest,
Jesus is there, a present guest.
I see them bowed with holy fear,
As if no eye but God's were near,
While they assume the vows of life
Ever to live husband and wife.
By all that's sacred in those names
Their hearts are lit with purest flames.
God's will in all things they obey,
The angels light about their way.
Like olive plants their children rise
And with their parents gain the skies.

As coming from the mountain down,
All nature wears a deepening frown.
Two wretches travel on their way,
Defiled in every breath they draw,
These vile contemners of God's law!
"Are not our lips our own?" they say,
"Who is the Lord we should obey?"
They took on them the marriage vow,
At Moloch's altar see them bow.
Into his burning arms they sent
Their offspring! Justice's bow is bent!
The sword that's hanging o'er their head
Is now with vengeance white,
Insulted nature cuts the thread,
Their sentence is not light,
They're turned to wolves, they're both accursed,
And both for blood forever thirst.

O all ye lightnings, from your place,
Fall on th' abominable race!
They have no right on earth to live
Who no such right to others give,

Consume them with your flashes bright,
Ashes to ashes, night to night.

THE GATES OF HELL AJAR.

BOOK IV.

Lo! the Destroyer's on his way!
What shall I of the doctors say
Who make this business a profession,
And profit by the great transgression?
If there is mercy out of hell
There is no mercy in it,
And I am very sure you are
Both dead and damned this minute.

What though you to the church belong,
And sing amidst the choir,
Upon your brow the seal is set
Of everlasting fire.

The foremost at the sunday school,
And in the house of prayer,
You've stepped your feet within hell's gate,
And know not that you're there.

Pile all the clouds from all the skies,
Mountains on mountains, let them rise
In one vast column high ;
Bid all the lightnings congregate,
Those startling ministers of fate,
And from their bosoms fly !
They could not tell so much of wrath
As waits upon the wretch's path
Who dares God's law defy.
And they who publish through the land
What lips may not repeat,
But which the crafty understand,
Kneel down at Satan's feet.
And all who sell or give consent
To use it for this vile intent,
Ingredient or instrument,
Due punishment shall meet.
Or else there is no law divine,
There is no judgment seat ;
And sin may have its holiday,
The Bible is a cheat.

To all the noble, dauntless band,

Physicians who for honor stand,
And smite the desolating hand
That would destroy life's sacred spring,
I bring you a thank-offering.
Your names are up to heaven sent,
As stars which gem the firmament.

I had a dream, I tell it here,
It was not all a dream I fear,
I looked into a charnel house,
To see what I should see,
Myriads of little children's eyes
Were looking up to me!
Why are these little children here?
A voice was whispered in my ear:
"They're sent from earth by hands unclean"
No father and no mother seen.
Where are their parents? then I cried,
An awful shriek from hell replied.
'Twas then I heard an angel blow
His trumpet long and loud,
For all the fowls of heaven to come
And fatten on their blood,

Who had on earth such monsters grown,
Not to have mercy on their own,
To wrest the sceptre from the hand of God.

Not adders with their poisonous breath,
Encoiled in venomed place,
So saturate the air with death
As that infestuous race,
Who scorn the blessings of the womb,
To make themselves a living tomb.
No language is invented yet,
Nor sword of truth so keenly whet,
As to reveal their doom.
Naught but the fiery tongue of hell
Can half their shame and vileness tell.
The cast-off serpent's hollow skin
Has more of conscience left within.
If there is found a darker spot,
Set on the soul a deeper blot,
Ye winds of heaven, tell it not!

A vision came into my thought,
Of all the ages, nations, brought

Before the judgment throne ;
A clear and strict account to give
In the full sight of all who live,
Of deeds which they had done.
Myriads of angels took their stand,
Each in his place at God's command,
To write down every word.
Darkness no longer was a screen,
And every deed of earth was seen,
And every thought was heard.

The congregated world was there,
Captains and mighty men,
Both small, and great, and rich, and poor,
Not one was absent then.
At God's right hand the righteous stand,
And I beheld the great white throne,
And Him who sat thereon,
Angels, archangels, and the just,
But all the rest were gone.

"Where are those multitudes," I said,
"Those multitudes of men?"

Now, looking through the gates ajar,
I saw them all again.

And murderers and thieves were there,
And haters of the good,
They who God's holy law despised,
A mixed and motley brood.

And all the crimes from Adam down,
Were in procession led;
And Abel's blood was crying still,
As on the day 'twas shed.

False witnesses and covetous,
And gamblers in their place,
And evil things which to the world
Had never shown their face.

Dishonest men who wore a mask
To hide their vile intent,
And mothers who contemned the care
Of children to them sent.

Sultans and richly crowne'd kings
Were there among the meanest things,
For only holiness has wings
To rise above this dismal sphere,
Where all the dregs of time appear.

There vengeance, which had waited long,
Stood ready to repay
The countless catalogue of wrong,
That on the earth held sway,
And none could find a hiding place,
But justice met them face to face.

Slave-holding preachers, a great band,
With Bible and with lash in hand,
The basest men that walk the earth,
Who claimed to be of heavenly birth,
With words of prayer upon their tongue,
But David's harp was all unstrung.
They bound the young lambs of their flock,
And sold them on the auction block !
Showing no pity, none is shown,
A chain of fire is round them thrown !

False ministers of every sort
Were here to clear inspection brought,
Not now before admiring eyes
Transformed to angels of the skies.

The glorious sun will always tell
The hour that it is bade,
God's balances are just as true,
In which our works are weighed.

Liars were there in foremost place,
As children of the devil,
And capable to rise apace
To any form of evil.

And heartless wrongs and cruelties,
And things too vile to name,
Were seen their due reward to reap
In everlasting shame.

And selfish men who sought their own,
Reckless of others' right,

Were made to see themselves alone,
With an inverted sight.

There was a crime enwrapped in flame,
Which stalked on earth devoid of shame.
A father who forsook his own,
And left the injured one to bear,
Alone, the burden he should share,
Of honor he had none.
Who hurled his offspring to its fate
By plea of illegitimate,
A moral skeleton!
The world around you'd scarcely see
A baser, meaner scamp than he.
Among the saints he once was seen,
Now a great gulf is fixed between.

Lawyers were there so full of brass,
Which they for gold had sought to pass,
Smothered in smoke of their own lies;
But honorable lawyers rise,
Arrayed in ermine pure and white,
Admitted to the courts in light!

Doctors, I blush to call their name,
So damned to infamy and shame,
With infants' blood upon their breast.
'Tis only now of these I speak,
But honor to the rest.

Yet still one lower depth was found,
Which reach of plummet could not sound,
A preacher, as a doctor taught,
By whom this murderous work was wrought.
Condemned alone in night to dwell,
Not seen but heard aloud in hell.

All who approve or lend their aid
When such vile deeds are done,
Which cover earth with grimmest shade
And obscurate the sun,
Though they may pass as stoutest saints,
Are murderers every one.

Gathered within the lowest cell,
To drink the bitterest cup of hell,
Mothers! who had their offspring slain!

The sword of justice, very bright,
Within those walls the only light,
Revealing every stain.

Their souls with blood were crimsoned o'er,
Pale were their faces as of yore,
And some that I had seen before
But would not see again !

Then as I turned mine eyes away
Another horror rose.
My guardian angel had me stay
Until the vision close.
A man, who had not long been dead,
Was standing on his hands and head
Condemned to use his feet no more,
But always look upon the floor !
"What has this creature done," I said,
The angel told his story o'er ;
An artless woman he deceived,
Promised to marry ; she believed,
A child was presently conceived.

To cover his and her dishonor
He thrust his nostrum drugs upon her,
These failing all to do the deed
A surgeon came in time of need.
Money was offered without stint,
The doctor took a lively hint,
And promised that he would succeed.
The girl was found among the dead,
The matter hushed, but little said.
Awhile the traitor walked in pride
The girl for mercy loudly cried.
The waters parted for her feet,
She treads upon the meadows sweet.
God took her where no murderers go,
But lilies blossom white as snow !
"His punishment is right," you'll say,
My guide took wings and flew away.

I saw a glimpse of heaven,
And fell upon my face.
To mortals 'tis not given
Such glorious things to trace.

A shining way led to its gate,
'Twas very narrow, very straight,
No beast of prey that path shall press,
It is the way of holiness.

If we make honor, wealth or fame,
Pleasure, or praise, our loftiest aim,
Be sure that we shall rise no higher
Than that to which our hearts aspire,
But if we would attain the best,
In thought, and word, and all we do,
God's glory we shall keep in view ;
Angels strike no higher string
When they serve, or when they sing,
And glorious will be our rest.

I have a message to the church,
And wish that it may know,
The pearl of truth is of great price,
And should be treated so.
Truth emanates from God alone,
And is a partner of His throne.
Where'er the precious germ is found

We loose our shoes, 'tis holy ground.
Religion is its beauteous flower,
And has a world-transforming power,
Yet much there is which bears the name,
That does not share its sacred flame,
It lifts us not to heavenly places,
It shineth not with elect graces.

Fear God, and His commandments keep,
Is man's whole duty given,
The golden key that never fails
To ope the gates of heaven.

The law is holy, just and good
That's set before mankind,
That we should love the Lord, our God,
With all our heart and mind,
It is the door to heaven's bliss,
We cannot enter without this.
'Tis heaven itself, as we are taught,
Within the soul is heaven wrought.

Obedience is the one great test,
As clearly in the Word expressed,

Life's tree, whereon all fruits are found,
And which with healing leaves is crowned.
Whatever we religion call,
Apart from this, is stubble all,
Whatever bears not on this point
Is spurious, and out of joint.

As Jacob's ladder touched the star,
Whence angels stepped their feet,
Descending from the realms so far,
To earth with errand sweet.
So on the bars of light we rise,
God's precepts bright, to gain the skies.

Concerning prayer, I'd speak a word,
For thereunto my soul is spurred,
"I do not like to hear folks talk,
I'd rather hear them pray.
Our wants so many and so great,"
I heard a person say.
So Baal's priests all day besought,
And yet the day no answer brought,
Elijah's prayer scarce moved the air

Before the sacred fire was there.
Does God within the heart inspire
A prayer, He'll answer the desire,
Or if He should the thing withhold,
For silver, He will send us gold.
Before we call He'll answer give,
While we're yet speaking we receive.
"I thank Thee, Father, Thou hast heard,"
Said Jesus when His heart was stirred.
And Lazarus from the grave awoke,
But not one word of prayer was spoke.

It is for lack of faith we stand
Such meager Christians in the land.
Faith works by love souls to refine,
Humanity becomes divine.
And when the church shall pay more care
To Sinai's law and less to prayer,
To faithless prayer, the work of art,
Like a stuffed bird without a heart,
Her face shall shine with clearer flame,
As Moses', when from God he came.

Unceasing prayer to us is given,
We breathe the air and song of heaven.

Why has the church so little hold
Upon mankind to-day?
Dim is become the most fine gold,
And truth is cast away.
Cross bearing, self-denial stand
As bygone ruins in the land.

From everybody's lips we hear,
There were conversions ten
Or ten times ten, wait but a year,
And count the number then.
False lights are flashing all around,
To make the darkness more profound.
Such words as these fall on our ear,
"Sir, were you saved when you came here?"
"No!" "Are you saved now?" "I am," then
Preacher and people shout, "Amen!"
Religion is so travestied—
Its beauty and its life have fled.

Yet there are many thousands left,
As hidden in the rock's deep cleft,
And ministers that I could name,
Of high example and pure fame,
Who preach the Word to you and me—
In truth and in sincerity. '

" Enjoy religion ? " What a phrase !
Invented in these modern days,
Where selfishness sits on the throne,
And men live to themselves alone.
The question ask, do we delight
To keep God's holy law in sight ?
And do we haste to turn our feet
Unto His testimonies sweet ?

When we for God and His great truth
Shall all our powers employ,
In everything there flows a spring
To us of holy joy.

And every lion that we slay,
In fierce temptation's hour,

When we again shall pass that way,
Shall yield us sweetness, power,
And from the cloud o'erspread with fears
Will fall a golden shower,
And still the bud bedewed with tears
Infolds the perfumed flower.

We shall be clothe'd with the sun,
The moon beneath our feet,
The dust of earth we tread upon
Shall be as heaven's street.

I tell a little anecdote,
Or rather I tell two,
Of facts which to my knowledge came,
And every word is true.
A man of years mature declared
That he in Christ's religion shared,
And gave as proof, that he had felt
Horrors on horrors, when he knelt.
The ground before his eyes would part,
As from a crater's brink, he'd start,
He had no rest at night.   Remorse!

His bedstead trotted like a horse?
Praise God, he said full fifty times,
If counted 'twere a hundred,
And tears were shed, and songs were sung,
And all the people wondered.
A cordial fellowship displayed,
Within the church awhile he stayed,
And this is all I need to tell,
Though many other things befell.

Another picture less forlorn,
A young man to the church was drawn,
Well known, and of a life so fair
That he was deemed example rare.
Before the church he told his story,
How he had sought the path to glory,
With joy he read the Holy Word,
And daily prayed before the Lord.
The deacons kindly heard him through,
And with the church held conference:
" No doubt what he has said is true,
But where is his experience?"
The preacher silently had listened,

His eyes with light of heaven glistened,
"The brother's in the way, we see,
How he came there is naught to me!"
And in this judgment all agree.
He scarcely ate his morning fare
Till he had sent the poor a share.
Long life he lived, by all admired,
And like the setting sun retired.

I tell another, not a fact,
Which yet displays the truth intact,
Five persons ask for prayer, may be,
The people stare and watch to see,
Which one will be the first to say,
"I know my sins are washed away!"
Three of the number came out bright,
The two remaining saw no light.
In twenty years they both are found,
Of life sincere, in doctrine sound.
The other three, who shone out so,
Have left the church long time ago.

I asked a doctor on a day,
A man religious, as we say;

In which there was most quackery,
In medicine or religion? He
Answered quickly, "Now you've got me."

Not in the whirlwind, or earthquake,
Did God unto Elijah speak,
He cometh not by observation,
His hidden ones are a great nation.

First the blade, and then the ear,
Is Bible language very clear.
Hindoo juggler makes us see
Spring up the full bearing tree.
Perfection which comes in a day
In far less time will pass away.
So Jonah's gourd grew in a night,
But withered when the sun was bright.

There was a tree which God had made,
It cast around a pleasant shade,
A thrifty tree, and towering high
It spread its boughs upon the sky.
Full many a year had rolled around

Since it was planted in the ground,
A seed, a germ, a little thing,
Now birds among its branches sing !
It withers not, its leaf is green,
Kingdom of heaven herein is seen.

Go through, go through, prepare the way,
We hear the voice prophetic say,
Take up the stumbling blocks, and show
The path my people's feet should go.
"Lift up the standard," saith my God,
"Spread all its lofty folds abroad."

Who is the light of this dark world,
And witness for the Truth ?
It is the living church of God,
Indued with heavenly youth.
But now thou art a lamp despised,
Thy beauty to the world disguised,
Yet there are gems upon thee set,
Jerusalem, I'll not forget.
And I of thee will sweetly sing
When God again shall Zion bring.

Talk not about the loving fold,
And Jesus' arms, while beasts you hold,
And while your skirts are red with stains
Of blood which flows from infant veins.

You say I knew it not, no doubt,
Then, why did you not search it out?
And will the church consent to bear
A scar the heathen would not wear,
And send its messengers abroad,
To teach them of the ways of God?

Honor to whom honor's due,
Church of Rome, I honor you,
In that you claim to hold a ban
Over this soul destroying clan.
And every church is struck with death
That suffers it to draw its breath.

A serpent stole an egg away,
In which a half-hatched fledgling lay,
Then coiled itself around the nest,
That serpent lies upon your breast!

Who careth for the wolves that prowl
About the church's door,
Or the hyena's dismal yawl
That's heard upon its floor?

Blow, blow ye the trumpet in Zion,
The solemn assembly call,
Ye ministers, weep at the altar,
Ye priests, on your faces fall.

His floor He will thoroughly purge,
His wheat He will gather in,
But He, with unquenchable fire,
Shall burn up the chaff of sin.

Else there is no cloud upon Sinai,
And there are no thunders heard,
There is no heat in its lightnings,
No truth in God's holy Word.

I thank Thee, Father, Thou hast made
The way so narrow, straight,
The way of life, the shining way,
That leads to heaven's gate.

O watchmen, standing on the walls,
Cry out and never cease,
Till down the streets the river runs,
Of righteousness and peace.

Dost thou teach us? perhaps you say;
"A little child shall lead the way."
Reproof is like a ring of gold,
To an obedient ear, we're told.

I said unto a minister,
Of standing and good fame,
Letters D. D., whate'er that be,
Were added to his name,
"Why preach you not against a thing
Which curses church and world?"
"Within three months," he said to me,
"I'd be from pulpit hurled."

I spake to a salvationist,
A general, called such,
"That is a thing," he answered me,
"Our workers cannot touch."

Religion thus on every side
Into contempt is brought.
The salt that has its savor lost
Is henceforth good for naught.

I thank the Lord that once there lived
A prophet who had zeal,
Who girded up his loins and ran
To entrance of Jezreel.

A woman, who high life sustained,
And all the preachers entertained,
Summoned a doctor to her aid.
And promised he should be well paid.
"How could you think of such a deed,
Who in the church's ranks take lead?"
"What do I care for that?" she said,
The doctor from her presence fled.
She who the laws of heaven defied
Herself of inward cancer died.

Here is a fact which I will state,
A fact too painful to relate,

For frightful things have frightful ends,
When one with nature's law contends.
An idiot, deformed and wild !
The means had failed to kill the child.
Secluded in a hidden room,
Beneath a costly, gilded dome,
By nurse attended all the while,
It does not see a mother's smile.
You'll say "her soul is rent with woes,
Her cup with anguish overflows."
In fashion's court she rules a queen,
The gayest 'mongst the gayest seen.

Oh ! could I lift my voice so far,
I'd call on every listening star,
To turn itself into a frown,
And flash its indignation down.
I'd call upon each blackening cloud
To break its thunders long and loud.
I'd call upon the church to wake,
And from its hand this viper shake
Into the flame from whence it came,
Into the ever-burning lake.

False, false religion, thee I hate,
Though thou may'st wear a crown of state.
Since Roman Church had power to slay,
Go count its victims, if you may.
Christians, like sheep, to mountain driven
And slaughtered in the face of heaven;
"Slay all, for God will know his own,"
Said the proud legate from his throne,
When beautiful Basyrus prayed
The hand of vengeance might be stayed.

Think of the iron virgin's breast,
With horrid prongs and teeth,
In which the heretics were pressed
Till they had ceased to breathe.

Indulgences were sold or given,
That vilest ones might enter heaven,
And Protestants have naught to say
While church prelatical held sway,
And the proud bishop offered thanks
When ears were shorn away,
And witnesses for Holy Truth

In cheerless dungeons lay.
See Pilgrims driven from their home,
And Puritans to Boston come ;
And here I'd gladly draw the curtain,
But truth must sound its trumpet certain.

Through all the shuddering ages down,
We scarcely find a blacker stain
Than settled on that famous town
Where Quakers were like cattle slain.
Their tongues with redhot irons bored
By these meek servants of the Lord !
The virus through the nation spread,
As spider cancer from its head.

O pure religion, undefiled,
Arrayed in garments white,
Thou humble, holy, heavenly child,
How art thou hid from sight !

And strong delusions then were sent,
The shepherds slew their sheep,
Witches unto the gallows went,
Such harvest sin doth reap.

A sample small may serve for all,
Judge sat upon his bench,
Before the judgment seat was brought
Candy—a negro wench.

"When did you become a witch?"
Judge asked in tone severe,
"Me no witch in Barbadoes,
"Me witch since I came here."

"Who made you a witch, tell me?"
Said judge, with question handy.
"Mistress gave me pen and ink,
Then I's witch," said Candy!

Burroughs who was a little man,
Held out a gun-barrel straight,
Which larger people could not do,
The gallows sealed his fate ;
And Cory, sad to tell, was crushed
Beneath the murderous weight.

But why revive these things to-day
When the dark cloud has passed away?

'Tis sin itself that I would slay ;
And wheresoe'er the beast is found,
I'd give his head a deadly wound.
Too long the world has borne the rod
Of false religion and false God.

And must I plead with you to show
That murder is a crime,
When Abel's blood is crying so,
And has been through all time?

And if there is one baser thing
Which can to light be brought,
It is, I deem, the murderous deed
That is in secret wrought.

Nor do I hate the sin,
And love the sinner well,
The heart in which such thought could spring
Is tinder box of hell.

"You must forgive," we hear one say,
"As for forgiveness you would pray."
Does God forgive impenitence?

Wise men will draw a lesson thence ;
Nor does He ask that we should be
More just, more pure, more wise than He.
'Tis that we have no proper sense
Of right, and wrong, that we dispense
Our pardons everywhere around,
Like Tetzel, whitening all the ground.

Sure justice will not be delayed,
Unless Almighty God
Shall nullify the law He's made
And throw away His rod.
Angelic hosts look down meanwhile
To greet repentance with a smile.

Church, in the wilderness, arise,
Drink from salvation's wells,
And let the notes of holiness
Ring out from all thy bells.

Where is the Lord God of Elijah,
And where is his mantle to-day?
The waters shall part at its waving,
To make for his people a way.

The sun shall awake at the dawning
From his chamber in the east,
The seal of a brighter morning
Shall glow upon thy breast.
Decked with salvation and beauty, thy banner
Shall float to the breeze and earth shout
    hosanna.

"I'll dwell in them and walk in them,"
So says His Holy Word,
And they shall be My people all,
And I will be their God.

But when the Son of Man shall come
Will He find faith on earth?
There seems to be but little room
For things of heavenly birth.

No room for Jesus in the inn,
No place that it could lend!
But of th' increase of His kingdom
And glory there's no end.

III

A handful there shall be of corn,
On top of mountain strown,
The fruit thereof abundantly,
Shall shake as Lebanon.

So like the stars for multitude,
When Gabriel's trump shall sound,
"Awake, ye dwellers in the dust,"
The faithful will be found.

They that are brought before the king,
His glory to behold,
Their raiment is of needlework,
Their clothing of wrought gold.

Put now thy beauteous garments on,
No more shall the unclean,
Or lion's whelp, or ravening beast,
Within thy gates be seen.

Of Zion it shall still be said,
That this man was born there,

This and that man, when God shall count,
He'll write in letters fair.

Go walk our city round about,
O ye anointed ones,
Mark well her towers and palaces,
And tell it to your sons.

Salvation shall our God appoint,
For walls and bulwarks strong,
The righteous nation enter in
With gladness and with song.

THE GATES OF HELL AJAR.

BOOK V.

O sacred muse, lift up my song,
With fiery words inflame my tongue,
That I of sin may sound the knell,
And wrap it in the sheet of hell,
This sin that has no parallel!
Ye sparkling orbs that o'er us roll,
Pure emblems of the human soul,
In which God flashes out the light
That cometh from the fountain bright,
Speak of His wondrous fame,
Your Maker, mine, who bids us shine,
His glory to proclaim.

When earth refreshed awakes from night,
To hail the footsteps of the light,
Do not the little drops of dew
Clearly display each heavenly hue?

God opens unto us the book
In which the hovering angels look
For lessons bright, for lessons true.
O truth immortal, at thy feet
I offer homage, tribute meet.
And I have offered praise to love,
A wave of glory sent,
To make this world like that above,
Revealing God's intent,
And sought out fittest words to tell
Its praise, which doth all praise excel.
And I have also sung of hate,
And hold it to my breast,
As love's celestial corollate,
A glory there impressed,
A gem of light on earthly ground,
In heaven more bright it may be found!
Pillars of truth which God has reared,
To show His law must be revered,
Else light and darkness were one thing,
We could not watch for the day spring.

Do we have fellowship with God

And Jesus Christ, His Son?
Though through the veil we dimly see,
Our heaven is here begun.
He that of glory never sings
Is like a Dodo without wings.
We shall not speak of trials, fears,
The world is brightest gemmed with tears;
We walk upon the mountains high,
Where prophets' feet have trod,
We drink the waters from the rock
Smitten by Moses' rod.

The sun gives glory to the field,
God is to us a sun and shield,
The rays of light that come to me
No other eye but mine can see.
Thus while o'er all His care extends,
A special care to each he lends.

For His great truth shall we not feel?
The Savior was consumed with zeal.
Humility takes foremost place,
And boldness follows, Christian grace.

First our obedience must be shown,
Then our revenge for sin made known,
To smite it with a two-edged sword,
Such honor have the saints of God.

Tell of the widow's funeral pyre,
And the grim wheels of Juggernaut!
Before us burns more cursed fire
Than ever entered Hindoo thought.
A Gorgon race of Christian name
Invent the crime and fan the flame.
It is against this sin I cry,
And blood cries louder far than I
Into the ears of the Most High.

Ye servants of the living God,
Who go at His command,
To publish all His truth abroad
To every creature, land,
Have you no word, have you no voice,
Have you no heart, no hand?
Who sees the sword, and does not warn,
For him the lifted sword is drawn.

Prepare for war ; the foe is come !
Not with the noise of hoof or drum,
But like the stealthy beast of prey,
That takes the tender lamb away !
What hand shall write their awful doom
Who throw the infant of the womb
Into the wolf's terrific jaws?
Defiant, trampling on God's laws,
And say that they have done no wrong,
And sing with you Zion's sweet song.

Have I no right in Jesse's son,
That I such things should look upon,
Which cover earth with hell's dark cloud,
And not lift up my voice aloud?
O sin, thou art a lightning-rod
Which draweth down the wrath of God
His word you handle with deceit,
To strike at small sins, fondle great.
If 'neath your smiles souls sink to hell
Shall you in heavenly mansions dwell?
To look on crime without a frown
And thereby give consent,

Would hurl from heaven an angel down
As quick as Satan went.

A horror lurks within the land,
By the foul breath of devils fanned ;
Earth would rend wide to take it in,
And press it to its burning center
Where not a ray of light could enter,
If earth could grasp so much of sin !
And yet it stands in holy place,
And flaunts defiance in your face,
Of insolence th' impersonation,
And the quintessence of damnation.
Since it defies Almighty God,
Shall it not hold for you a rod ?
And will you cringe beneath its ban ?
Be strong and show thyself a man !
He that is weak, armed with the truth,
Shall be like David in his youth,
And he that is as David be,
As God, as a strong angel he ;
Strong in His name to whom is given
All power in earth, all power in heaven.

Fight not as those that beat the air
Like Polyphemus!   Hit somewhere.
E'en the sun's rays would not be bright
Did they upon no object light.
Nor need you wonder if the shafts
Of sin be thickly plied.
You are not greater than your Lord,
Saviors are crucified.
Through suffering we gain the right
To walk upon the pavement bright,
To walk with Him in raiment white,
Who trod the winepress here alone,
And now is seen amidst the throne.
Ye lightnings, from your pillows leap,
Arouse, ye thunders, from your sleep,
God has a controversy here ;
And He will make His judgment clear ;
Nor shall His sword return invain,
Drunk with the blood of many slain.
This scorpion's sting, this vulture's beak,
This crime of crimes of which I speak !
Banish your gospel from the land,

Call home your missionary band,
Or take the word of truth in hand.

No longer after shadows run,
But turn about and face the sun!
Show yourselves worthy of your station,
As Christian leaders of a nation.
Strike this great evil at the root,
Not with a penknife cut the shoot
And just enough to make it flourish,
And thus the deadly Upas nourish!
If there had been no other sin
There'd be a hell to take this in.

Curse Meroz, curse him bitterly,
Because he stayed behind,
And all who come not up shall be
As chaff before the wind.

Still let the word of exhortation
Fall on the ears of your vocation,
Descent is easy from the skies,
Not so among the stars to rise.

I think I speak the truth in love,
But yet I too must faithful prove.
There is a reason we may guess,
Why men so readily transgress.

Religion's face is scarcely seen
Through the dark veil that is between.
Hence to the world its heavenly light
Is almost lost, and often quite.
That angel sweet, sent from the skies,
To guide our feet to Paradise.
An angel false appears in sight!

Faith for good works is substituted,
And by it every sin commuted,
Until the church is foremost found
To tread upon forbidden ground.
And the pure gospel comes to be
The maelstrom of iniquity.
Who pierced you with the keenest blade?
The one who high profession made.
Who took your money, weight in gold,
For paper that he would not hold?

Who dug for you the deepest pit,
Intending you should fall in it?
Who told to you the blackest lie?
I think I need not make reply.
Who followed you with fiercest wrath,
As lion rampant on your path?
Held o'er your head the vengeful ban?
It was the high religious man.

Christianity, that glorious plant,
That plant of high renown,
By thoughtless feet and impudent
Alike, is trodden down.
And selfishness has taken place
Of honor, justice, truth and grace.
The thunderings have fled away,
The sky on Sinai's clear to-day.
Where there's no law there's no transgression.
Herein, perhaps, we find the key
To half the holiness we see.
In those who make a bold profession
That they have in a moment gained
That which St. Paul had not attained.

A righteous life's of small account,
The leopard walks the holy mount.

I will relate an anecdote,
And many such there are afloat.
Straws show which way the wind is blowing
And little things have a great showing.

A woman prayed so eloquent
'Twould seem it were an angel sent
To lift us from terrestrial sphere
Up to the gates of heaven near.
Each word mellifluous, loftier swells,
As chiming with celestial bells.
Thence to her rural home she came,
And with her gun took steady aim,
As sitting in an easy chair,
To shoot down robins, one, two, three,
That lighted on a cherry tree,
And made sweet music there.
A neighbor, a samaritan,
A plain, kind-hearted, honest man,
Offered these words unto her ear :

"Who made the birds, and bade them sing
The praises of creation's King?
Who spreads your table with rich food,
Shall He not feed His little brood?
How could you break their handsome wing?"
The woman met him with a sneer,
"They sha'n't have my cherries," she said,
Another robin fell down dead.

Luther, that one-eyed giant, rose,
A thousand evils to oppose,
To set religion in true light!
Yet robbed it of its garments white.
To soil the truth which God has given
Would shut an angel out of heaven.

"Sin boldly," still we hear him say,
"Believe! but you need not obey."
Moses is to perdition sent,
His law, and the Old Testament.
The seamless robe of Christ is rent!
The serpent that once spoke to Eve
Was not more potent to deceive.

No wave of absolution free,
Like this, e'er flowed from Papal See,
And still it flows the world around
Till in it church and world are drowned.
John Wesley taught no better creed,
I quote them both that all may read.
Now men may lie with pious unction,
God's laws defy without compunction.
The great red dragon with his tail,
That did the stars of heaven assail,
And ready to devour,
That once before the woman stood,
And after her cast out a flood,
Had no such deadly power !
Is Christ the minister of sin ?
Let judgment at God's house begin,
From spot or wrinkle they're made free
Who shall the King in beauty see !

O blessed, pure and spotless life,
That's honored by the Lord,

---

* See appendix.

Childhood and youth, manhood and age,
Obedient to His word !
This is the right, the royal road,
That leads up to the throne of God.
I still must keep the truth in sight,
Although the word upon you light,
Which, as you stand in holy fear,
You may be very glad to hear.

O truth ! lift up thy mighty voice,
As a strong angel sent,
Till from the face of people all,
The covering be rent.

Search all the sermons you have preached
Within the past ten years,
See if a precept of the Word
In any text appears,
Or "Golden Rule," from heavenly source,
Is made the theme of your discourse.

"Look not each one upon his own,
But on another's wealth,"

The rule that strikes at selfishness,
Promoting moral health.

How many people in the land
Have thought to practice this command,
Or held it closely to their heart,
As of their duty forming part?

With conscience seared, or none at all,
Men low at mammon's feet do fall,
Deceive in measure or in weight,
And wholesome food adulterate.

"Trade and religion are two things,
Young man, I'd have you know."
So said a deacon who had bought
A widow's goods too low.
The whole head's sick, the whole heart's faint,
Deliver me from such a saint.

Who gains the most, no matter how,
Is sure to win the lowest bow.
And saint the sinner will excel,
If you the difference can tell.

Christ had nowhere to lay his head,
Elijah was by ravens fed.
In ceremonies you are strict,
In Christian conduct derelict.

Think not I throw my arrows round,
As shot from bow too free,
Better from friend receive a wound,
Than kiss from enemy.

Have honor and a holy life
Lost all their sweet perfume,
That they should be consigned by you
To darkness and the tomb?
That heartlessness and villainy
Should wear the loftiest plume.

Half the defaulters in the land
Are stalwarts of the praying band,
They'd sleep upon the orphan's bed,
But not until their prayers they'd said.
" Do we not to the church belong?
What we shall do cannot be wrong."

'Tis thus the desert Bedouin
Kneels down at break of day,
Prays Allah send some Christian dog
For him to rob and slay.

I tell a story, false or true,
It serves the end I have in view.
A man was murdered for a dime!
And one there was confessed the crime.
Court asked, "What did you get beside?"
"His dinner-pail," the wretch replied.
"What else?" "In it some bread and meat,
The bread, your honor, 'twas I ate,"
"And did you not the meat partake?"
"I could not, sir, for my soul's sake;
The meat and sure I threw away,
I'm not allowed it on fast day!"

There was a time in Rome, 'tis said,
When not a man was found
But to the faith was infidel,
To ceremonies bound,
Which like the brazen serpent all,

To human worship lowered,
May well be broken, cast away,
And Christ alone adored.

You call up men to be converted—
Bid them turn away from Sin!
Full long enough with truth we've flirted
On the foundation to begin.

There's no rebuke, none saith restore,
But prayers are offered by the score—
A marvelous experience told,
And heaven within your grasp you hold.
You need not walk the narrow way,
The road is broadened from that day.
Patient continuance in well doing
Is deemed a path not worth pursuing.
Religious technicalities
Are shams of the worst kind,
They neither renovate the heart
Nor benefit the mind.

Still there are those, as well you know,
Who cry out "blow the trumpet, blow,"

Who to hide their vile intentions,
Wear a cloak of wide dimensions
Inlaid with piety and song,
Sweet as e'er fell from mortal tongue.
They'd be in prison making shoes
If justice should get half its dues.
Though wolves into the fold may leap,
We may not call the wolf a sheep.
Defending truth, I boldly say,
Of crimes the foulest known to-day,
In their proportion, ten to one,
By so-called ministers are done.
Because they cast the law away
That's holy, good and just,
Their root shall be as rottenness.
Their blossom be as dust.

Vice is respected, canonized,
Goodness rejected and despised,
The libertine's in triumph led,
Petted and patted on the head,
" Poor fellow ! " is the worst word said.
"Come to the church," where all invite,

"You shall be made a Christian knight,"
And he is best who's loud to tell
How he has beat the paths to hell.
Religion is a burlesque made,
And sin becomes its stock in trade.

Say you, "we honor grace to show
How near the pit our feet may go?
As we repent we shall behold
The gates of pearl, the streets of gold."

No penitence for sin is found
In those who love its name to sound,
And they who listen with delight
Are smitten with a kindred blight.
The moral man the gauntlet runs,
He's shot at by a thousand guns.
Till one is raised to heights sublime
Who dare say virtue is no crime.

And he who says the law of God
Is something we should keep,
Is cast out of the gospel ship,
Like Jonah to the deep.

Do I dishonor truth divine,
That I would have its face to shine?
Fair as the moon, clear as the sun,
A light to lighten every one?
The Christian faith calls us to heed
God's will in thought, and word, and deed.

Religion is the basest thing
That ever shamed the earth
From which the graces do not spring,
Graces of heavenly birth,
A monster it stands forth confessed,
Face of a man, a beast the rest.

Oh! that there were a prophet heard,
Proclaiming forth the holy word!
As ocean lifts its waves on high,
The elements to purify!
A hand upon the wall to write!
Belshazzer's knees again would smite.

The prize of God's high calling,
Glory before us set,

Is that we be like Him in whom
Both God and man are met.

O sacred and pure is the law of the Lord,
And sweet are the voices that speak in His
 Word,
Where wisdom has mingled her choicest of
 wine,
He lives who shall drink from that fountain
 divine,
His soul with the nectar of heaven is fed,
His feet on the mountains of Bether are sped.

" 'Tis not by works, it is by faith,
That we reach heaven," disputer saith,
The faith is dead that is not blent
With virtue's holy element,
A ragged rock upon the sea,
And round it many wrecks there be.
But living faith's another thing,
And is of righteousness the spring.
It is the clear foundation stone
That every grace is built upon.

Preach faith forever, I will shout,
But leave not truth and honor out.
Avoiding Scylla, you've run in
To Charybdis, whirlpool of sin.

But character should like a flower
Unfold its petals fair,
And every part with all the parts
In symmetry compare.

You've praised the prodigal so long,
That one is almost driven
To be a prodigal himself,
That he may enter heaven.
While the churlish elder brother,
You with maledictions smother,
Forgetful of the father's words,
As told by lips divine :
"Thou'rt ever with me, O my son,
All that I have is thine."

To keep Thy precepts I made haste,
The royal psalmist said,

Sweeter than honey to my taste,
And by Thy word I'm fed.

Whatever things are lovely, pure,
Honest, of good report,
If there be any virtue, praise,
To these things give your thought,
'Twas thus the great apostle taught.

In the example Jesus set,
All beauty we shall see,
"And I, if I be lifted up,
Will draw all men to Me!"

A nobler type of piety,
So full of truth and grace,
With righteousness a breastplate,
Shall cheer the human race.

The mountain of God's house shall rise,
And take its lofty seat
Upon the top of mountains, where
Earth and the heavens meet.
All nations unto it shall flow!

The day that's hastening, as you know,
Shall like an oven burn,
When all the proud shall be laid low,
All who His truth shall spurn.
The Lord who cometh suddenly
Shall to His temple turn,
And He, the sons of Levi
Shall purify as gold,
And Judah offer pleasant things
As in the days of old.

Now let us walk in pastures green,
Where the skipping lambs are seen,
And the shepherd leads his flock
To waters gushing from the rock.
Roam in nature's gardens wild,
Drink from fountains undefiled ;
And as we wander here and there
Cull healing herb and floweret rare ;
The living, flying waifs of thought,
As butterflies in nets are caught.
Nature rears her mountains high,
Spreads the storm-clouds on the sky,

Bids the waves their message tell,
Tints the blossoms in the dell ;
Is in many voices heard,
Thunderclap and song of bird.

A picture of the human soul,
In which is read and found the whole.
Who has not seen a shallow stream
Foaming with noise to-day,
What time it waxeth warm, says Job,
It vanisheth away.
Religion the same story tells,
Still water is in deepest wells.

Not with our lips to make display,
But in our actions bright,
Unselfish actions shedding on
The world divinest light.

And beautiful the word of God,
By inspiration given,
Who adds thereto or takes therefrom
Hurts the pure wine of heaven.

When we do more than we should do,
We always something lack;
The cross that's brightest on the breast
Is lightest on the back.

I shall be pardoned, I am sure,
For praising Holy Writ.
"Thy word is very pure, therefore
Thy servant loveth it."

The Golden Rule is cast away
As worthless tin or brass to-day.
The sterling virtues that should grace
Our lives, have in our creeds no place.

And I will venture at some risk
To make a slight addition,
That all may note the novel sound,
And think of the omission.

"And I believe in righteousness,
As pleasing in God's sight,
In justice, truth and purity,
And meekness, virtues bright!"

" And I believe in the command
To do to every one
As we would have them do to us,
Till time's hour-glass is run."

We scarcely need a surer sign
That here we walk the ways divine,
Than that we hold another's right
Sacred and precious in our sight.

Do justly, love mercy, walk humbly with God,
That path which the saints in all ages have trod,
With the contrite in heart the Lofty One dwells,
And they shall drink water from heavenly wells.
Your creeds are all good as they tend to this goal,
Apart from all this they are chaff to the soul.

Living epistles we shall be,
True copies of His Word,
In which all those who look may see
The likeness of the Lord.

E'en as the varied tints of light
Combine to give the perfect white,

A type of holiness, I ween,
That is in nature's kingdom seen.
So let the bread of life be broken,
 By every word which God hath spoken,
To nourish, beautify the soul,
And make it in His image whole.
But darkness has no ray within,
And it may be a type of sin.
The Sun is chasing it away,
The glorious messenger of day!
Watchman, on thy lofty height,
What of the night, what of the night?
The morning cometh; without clouds!
The morning cometh, morning bright!

Prophetic glories, long foretold,
Are blushing in the east,
And on His mountain God shall make
For all the world a feast.

We rise above the whirling dust
Struck from the wheels of time,
We dwell in crystal palaces,
We walk the fields sublime.

Be bold for truth, again I cry,
Ye preachers, lift your voices high,
Wrest innocence from lion's paws,
And plead the glory of His laws
Who watches o'er the sparrow's nest ;
His prophets you will be confessed,
And you will be as angels bright,
Dwelling in God, for God is light.

'Twas when the priests had dipped their feet
In Jordan, Jordan did retreat.
Go forward at the voice of God
Like Moses with his lifted rod,
The waters will their Maker know,
And the Red Sea shall cease to flow !

THE GATES OF HELL AJAR

BOOK VI

How beauteous are their feet who stand
On Zion's hill, God's word in hand.
Of mercy, judgment, still they sing
No bird can fly upon one wing;
Who say to Herod, " 'tis not right,"
They shall be great in the Lord's sight.
Though they be clothed in camel's hair,
Wild honey, locusts, be their fare.

And now I raise my prayer to Him,
Who rules above, below,
That by the touch of Seraphim,
My lips may ever glow,
Prepared to tender wrath to crime,
And praise to holiness sublime.

The Savior of the world has prayed,
His people may be one,
And one in Him! Has He not said,
They shall sit in His throne.

What's bound on earth is bound in heaven,
Such power is to His servants given,
It is not by succession done,
It is that they with Him are one.

With trembling we are bade to see
The chambers filled with imagery.
Look, where the filthy satyrs dance
Around God's holy ordinance!
They the sweet flower of love despise,
That's left to us of Paradise.
And nurse a poisonous root instead,
With blood which their own hands have shed.
Abomination! Desolation!
They know not where their feet have trod,
They've trampled on the Son of God,
Their wine is the wine of Sodom,
Where they delight to dwell,

Their grapes are the grapes of Gomorrah
Where fire and brimstone fell !
Lot's wife we read was turned to salt,
But they are turned to sin,
She but one look at Sodom took,
Which they are living in.

I heard a voice from heaven cry,
Whom shall I send?   And who will be
The one to go ?   I said :   Send me.
O let some Seraph swiftly fly
With a live coal from altar brought,
My heart and lips to purify,
That I may speak the words I ought !
To say to all the heartless brood,
I damn you in the name of God !
From my right arm the lightnings go,
Which He has given me to throw,
Nor could I breathe the vital air,
If I should qualify or spare.
You've spurned His work, you've spurned His
    will,
And He with wrath your cup shall fill.

Which burneth to the lowest deep
In sorrow to lie down and weep.
Where the worm dieth not,
And the fire is quenched never,
And the smoke of their torment,
Ascends up forever!

The Son of God from heaven came
To glorify His Father's name :
The Father glorifies the Son,
In whom His will is always done.
'Tis in the human family
A type of heaven itself we see !

When vivid lightnings fall around
To magnify His name,
Whoever saw the secret place
From whence the lightnings came?

There is a great and dreadful God,
Who hides Himself to-day,
Before whose face the heavens and earth
And sea shall flee away.

Because there's wrath, we must beware,
And to His law pay strictest care.

It is our life that we obey
The law so holy, just and good,
For if we cast His law away
He cannot bless us if He would.
For the obedient alone
Is peace, and light, and gladness sown.

God is not mocked, we ought to know
That we shall reap as we shall sow.
Each sin though subtle as our thought
Will clearly to the light be brought.
And if our hearts condemn us not,
He may behold some secret spot.
And we have every need to cry,
Search us, O God, and purify.
We shall be lifted, it may be,
Upon a cross His face to see.

O foolish people and unwise,
How long will ye God's gifts despise,

While wisdom offers you her ways,
Riches and honor, length of days,
And bids you turn from every sin
To walk her pleasant paths within,
And angels pause on wings of light
To bear you upward in their flight,
And lightnings flash, and thunders peal,
Their Maker's glory to reveal?
Acquaint thyself with Him and be
At peace, His wings shall cover thee.

Happy, O Israel, art thou,
O save'd by the Lord,
Sword of thine excellency He,
And He thy great reward.

Now there appears before my view
A man of God, a preacher true,
He's standing up in heaven's defence,
He's clothe'd with Omnipotence.
Rubies are worthless in his sight
Compared with truth's diviner light.

To glorify his God is all,
Alike he honors great and small.
The flock of God with care he feeds,
And into pastures green he leads.
His soul is lit with heavenly charms,
He takes the young lambs in his arms,
Fired by the bright example set
Of Him who trod Mount Olivet.
Rightly divides the Holy Word,
That is to sin a two-edged sword,
And while he points he leads the way
To portals of celestial day.

O fair is the sun when he sinks to his rest,
And gathers in bright folds the clouds to his breast,
Of crimson and violet, purple and gold,
But fairer than all which the eye can behold
Is faith, the sweet faith, to mortals that's given
In Him who has brightened our pathway to heaven.

I thank my God for worlds on worlds
Of joy to us made known,
Above the glory of the sun
And brightness of the moon.
I thank Him for the glorious things,
O Zion, said of thee,
And for the waters of His truth,
Flowing to us so free,
That we are borne to heaven's port
Upon a level sea—
That we may sing, where is thy sting
O death ! O grave, thy victory !

In the dark cloud God sets His bow,
And writes His promise there ;
Which oft through tears is made to glow,
In letters doubly fair.
And all the cloud, if viewed aright,
Is filled for us with rainbows bright.

Oh ! that some quill from lofty wing
Were dipped in Helicon's pure spring,
And I with it were bade to tell,

Beauty which doth all praise excel !
A wife, the glory of her race,
A mother, glad to fill her place,
Leading her children to the Lord
By clear example and sweet word.
As angels here with folded wings,
Waiting to touch the heavenly strings !
Prudent and wise in her affairs,
Prayerful, yet without show of prayers.
Her heart with kindness overflows,
Dispensing mercy as she goes.
Her children rise and call her blest,
Her husband praises her as best.
And angels weave with sunset thread
The crown to place upon her head.

And I will bless the holy life
That's here to mortals given,
Sacred relation, husband, wife,
Foretaste and type of heaven.

I will extol the human soul,
The human soul divine,

In which God has His image set,
And made His glory shine.
As stars are in the heavens strown
We do not now behold,
Its infinite capacities
Shall evermore unfold.
And truth, and love, and beauty fill
Its palaces of gold.

O beauty, thou spreadest thy robe on the skies,
Thou lookest to us in the violet's eyes,
Thou art heard in the song that the forest birds
    sing,
Thou art seen in the spots on the butterfly's
    wing,
Thou sit'st on the white clouds that over us roll,
But thy home, thy sweet home, is found in the
    soul.

And love is beautiful indeed,
With joy celestial shod,
In which our hearts are made to read
The bosom thoughts of God.

I thank Him for beauty, I thank Him for love,
For blessings so freely sent down from above,
For shower and for sunshine to earth which are
    given,
And for the first fruits of His kingdom in
    heaven!
We watch for that city, its gates to behold,
Where God in His Son doth all beauty unfold,
Its wall is of jasper, its street is pure gold.

And still to beauty, love and truth
I would my song repeat,
And ask that in my heart they dwell,
Immortal, pure and sweet.

The soul that's filled with beauty's soul
In the divinest sense,
Is every whit from sin made whole,
Its vineyards are from thence.
Destroy it not, on holy ground,
A blessing in the cluster's found.

And I might sing of flashes rare,
Out from that diamond throne,
Of glimpses heaven could hardly spare,
Which unto me have flown,
And of my being form a part,
Glimpses of heaven within my heart!
Of fountains and of living springs
Which gush within the soul,
And of the bright and beauteous things
Which through my heart have stole.
Sparks of wisdom, wit refined,
Flowing from a star-lit mind,
Where dwell enthroned in lofty state
The royal virtues, love and hate.
Fitted together with such grace,
Magnificent without pretence,
And luminous with brightest sense,
A goddess born we clearly trace!
'Twas as if heaven had lent the mold
Immortal beauty to unfold.
Out shining in an open face
Beauty transcending speech or thought,
As heaven itself to earth were brought.

Glory with glory interwrought
As heaven itself did earth embrace !
I said, "ye are gods," and do not we
Herein our real greatness see ?
Why lie among the pots so long,
When for your lips there waits a song ?
And you may rise on wings of dove,
To chant the melodies of love !

O could I raise the loftiest note
That on the sea of time should float,
Whose ripples would forever be
The chorus of eternity,
I'd praise the beauty of sweet love,
Which links this earth with heaven above ;
I'd praise the beauty of sweet love,
And I would curse with the same breath
The crime that puts sweet love to death.
Prepared in heaven, ye lightnings keen,
Drive it into space unseen !

 In a radiant sphere,
  There's a heaven-lit isle,

Where the sun never sets,
And the flowers ever smile.
'Tis from thence the glad song
Of the angels we hear,
From that heaven-lit isle,
In the radiant sphere,
Saying, this is the bright,
The blissful abode
Of all those who delight
In the law of the Lord.
There the breath of the air
Is the fragrance of spring,
And the joy of that land
Is the sight of the King !

By every nation, people, tongue,
Shall the new song in heaven be sung,
And let the beauty of the Lord
Our God upon us rest,
As the pure touches of the sun
Are on the flowers impressed.
So shall the living seal of truth
Shine out upon our breast,

And we shall be to all who see
Light of the world confessed.

Why do we pray, some people say,
Since God knows all our need?
Because our life is part of His
And He has so decreed.
And He will also have us know
The source whence all our blessings flow.
On wings of prayer and praise we rise,
Where glory springs, but never dies.

Father in heaven, Creator, All,
Lo, at Thy feet I prostrate fall,
And offer with the heart's pure flame,
Thanksgiving, praise in Jesus' name,
For all the goodness Thou hast shown,
And for the love to us unknown,
And when temptation's power was strong,
I thank Thee for the conqueror's song.

What great deliverance hast Thou wrought
For those who trust in Thee,

They through affliction's might are brought
Thy face with joy to see.

And I will praise the glorious grace
Which Thou hast given to our race,
Of children who our image bear
And with us in life's blessings share,
And though their stay be transient here
Their voice is sweet in Jesus' ear.
O Shepherd of thine Israel,
Within Thy fold they ever dwell.

Twelve years of life Thou hast me lent
Since man's allotted days were spent,
And brightly glow, and brighter yet,
The lights in heaven's window set.

My soul, wait only upon God,
And wait unto the end,
That thou may'st reach His blest abode,
And to His throne ascend,
And let thy testimony shine,
As lamp that burneth clear,

In thought, in word, and deed divine,
For Him with holy fear
Who bids thee thrust sin's murderous hosts
With truth's well-pointed spear.

I saw a mighty angel stand,
One foot on sea, and one on land,
That there be no more time he swore.
Stay, stay, one moment I implore,
'Till all His saints within His hand,
All who are clothed in raiment white,
Whose brows by seraph's breath are fanned,
Shall call on God with all their might,
Call on His name, give Him no rest
Till earth be purified and blest.
The cloud of sin is rolled from sight!

Now shines the sun as seven days,
The moon sends forth her mellowest rays,
The Prince of Darkness takes his flight!
Fair, over sin and sorrow's tomb,
Shall whitest lilies bud and bloom!
All hail, thou morning bright!

Rejoicing stars are heard again,
As on creation's birthday, when
God said, let there be light.

FINIS.

A PRAYER.

O God, the Creator of heaven and earth, Omnipotent, Omniscient, whose name is Holy, Thou art a God of Judgment! By Thee actions are weighed. I thank Thee that Thou hast enabled me to lay this gift on Thine altar. Let the word prosper in the thing whereunto it is sent. Let it be as a fire and a hammer which breaketh in pieces, that this people may know that Thou art the Lord God, and that I have done all these things at Thy word. Vindicate Thy truth and glorify Thy name.

APPENDIX

[See page 127.] FROM LUTHER.

"The ten commandments do not belong to us Christians, but only to the Jews, we will not admit that any, the least precept, be imposed upon us. Therefore look that Moses be sent packing in malam rem—with a mischief, and that thou be not moved with any terror of him, but hold him suspected for a heretic, cursed and damned, and worse than the pope or devil."—[Works of Luther, Vol. I.]

"Be a sinner and sin boldly, sin cannot pluck us away from Him (the Lord) although we were to commit fornication or murder a thousand and a thousand times a day. A Christian cannot, if he will, lose his salvation by any magnitude or multitude of sin unless he ceases to believe, for no sin can damn him but unbelief alone."

Shall we call such teaching right, or boldly testify against it? Many Bible texts might be quoted to contradict these ravings of Luther, but one will be sufficient "Do we then make void the law of God through faith? God forbid; yea, we establish the law."

FROM WESLEY.

"How is Christ the end of the law for righteousness to every one that believeth? In order to understand this you must understand what law is here spoken of. And this I apprehend to be the Mosaic, the whole Mosaic dispensation—containing three parts, the moral, political and ceremonial. The Adamic law, that given to Adam in innocence, properly called the law of works. Christ is the end of the Adamic as well as the Mosaic law. By His death He put an end to both; He hath abolished both the one and the other, with regard to man, and the obligation to observe either the one or the other is vanished away. Nor is any man living bound to observe the Adamic or the Mosaic law."

The wonder is that they who listen to such teachings are not even worse than they are; the whole moral law is at once abrogated from men's conscience and thought. Christ said: "I came not to destroy the law or the prophets."

www.ingramcontent.com/pod-product-compliance
Lightning Source LLC
Chambersburg PA
CBHW030242170426
43202CB00009B/591